WORLD WAR II DAY BY DAY

D-DAY

1944

Charlie Samuels

BROWN BEAR BOOKS

BROWN BEAR BOOKS

Published by Brown Bear Books Ltd
4877 N. Circulo Bujia
Tucson, AZ 85718
USA

and
First Floor
9-17 St Albans Place
London N1 0NX

ISBN: 978-1-78121–040-6

Library of Congress Cataloging-in-Publication Data
available upon request

Editorial Director: Lindsey Lowe
Managing Editor: Tim Cooke
Design Manager: Keith Davis
Designer: Jerry Udall
Picture Manager: Sophie Mortimer
Children's Publisher: Anne O'Daly
Production Director: Alastair Gourlay

Manufactured in the United States of America

CPSIA compliance information: Batch#: AG/5507

Photographic credits:

Front Cover: Robert Hunt Library.
All photographs Robert Hunt Library.

Contents

Introduction

D-Day—June 6, 1944—was the day of decision in the war on Hitler's Germany. For a 24-hour period, the outcome of the conflict hung in the balance as the Allies launched one huge assault to land on the beaches of Normandy. If they could overcome the defenses of the Germans' Atlantic Wall, they would open a second front in Europe. If they failed, the blow to morale might have been catastrophic.

Allied priority

The risk of failure had to be reduced to a minimum. The invasion was therefore the result of 26 months of planning. It drew on innovative forms of amphibious warfare and inspired new technology: new forms of landing craft, specialized armored vehicles, and floating harbors, called Mulberry harbors.

At the first Anglo-American summit conference in Washington, D.C., in January 1942, British prime minister Winston Churchill and U.S. president Franklin D. Roosevelt had agreed that an invasion of occupied Europe and Germany should be the first priority of the new alliance. All Allied operations against Adolf Hitler's Third Reich were intended, ultimately, to lead to that end.

Strategic preparation

The defeat of the U-boat threat in the Atlantic Ocean during 1943 and 1944, for example, was necessary to allow the safe passage to Europe of more than 1 million U.S. troops and millions and millions of tons of arms and supplies for the invasion. The joint bombing campaign against Germany by the Royal Air Force (RAF) and the U.S. Army Air Force (USAAF) damaged the German ability to manufacture aircraft, forced the Germans to increase fighter production, and drew aircraft away from France to defend Germany. Even the invasions of Sicily and Italy in 1943 helped improve planning for large-scale amphibious operations and cooperation between land, sea, and air forces, and between the various Allied chains of command.

In a hail of enemy gunfire and artillery shells, U.S. soldiers surge onto Utah Beach early on D-Day.

U.S. GIs drag their comrades ashore after their landing craft was sunk off Utah Beach. Many soldiers drowned before even reaching the shore.

Despite the huge build-up in Allied forces, success could not be taken for granted. An unprecedented security operation was put in place to keep troop movements secret. Deception operations set out to convince the Germans that the inevitable invasion would come in Norway or the Balkans, or in the Pas de Calais in France. Instead, the invasion would target the beaches of Normandy.

For over four years, the Germans had been fortifying the French coast with barbed wire, beach obstacles, and concrete strongpoints. The "Atlantic Wall" was a formidable barrier. But Hitler was preoccupied with the Eastern Front, where the Soviet Union was gaining an upper hand over the German forces. He diverted resources east rather than west. Despite some late doubts among Allied commanders, who feared high casualty rates during an assault, it seemed by early 1944 that the invasion was coming closer.

Final planning

In December 1943, U.S. general Dwight D. Eisenhower was appointed Supreme Allied Commander. The next month, the British general Bernard Montgomery became commander of Allied ground forces. By now the planning for D-Day (the "D" simply stood for "day") was well advanced. The timescale from this point to the invasion—codenamed "Overlord"—was only five months.

The view from a British landing craft shows obstacles and debris on Gold Beach on D-Day.

A German sentry looks out from an artillery position on the French coast.

DECEMBER 7, Tunis
President Franklin D. Roosevelt stops in Tunisia on his way home from Allied conferences in Tehran and Cairo. He appoints General Dwight D. Eisenhower as Supreme Commander of the Allied Expeditionary Force.

DECEMBER 12, France
Field Marshal Irwin Rommel arrives in northern France to review defense preparations.

DECEMBER 19, France
Rommel meets with Field Marshal Gerd von Rundstedt. The field marshals agree that the Pas de Calais is the most likely invasion point.

DECEMBER 24, Great Britain
British General Bernard L. Montgomery of the Eighth Army is appointed commander of 21st Army Group. He will report to Eisenhower.

DECEMBER 27, Algiers
Montgomery flies to Algiers, North Africa, to meet Eisenhower to discuss the organization of the Allied armies for Operation Overlord.

DECEMBER 30, Italy
Montgomery leaves Eighth Army HQ in Italy for Great Britain and his new command.

DECEMBER 31, France
Rommel submits his first report to Hitler on likely Allied intentions for the invasion. He believes the Allies will strike near Boulogne and Calais, from where V-1 flying rockets are launched against London.

STRATEGY AND TACTICS: Deception plans

Operation Bodyguard was a large-scale exercise to hide the timing and location of the invasion from the Germans. It would also fool Hitler into dispersing his forces around Europe, so that when the invasion occurred there would be fewer troops in France to meet it. The deception was both military and diplomatic. Militarily, the Allies maneuvered to make it look as though the invasion would come around Pas de Calais in northern France, and that Norway and the Balkans would also be attacked. Diplomatically, the aim was to undermine Hitler's trust in his allies, by suggesting that Hungary, Romania, and Bulgaria might defect to the Allied side. That forced Hitler to keep more troops in the East rather than move them to strengthen the West. The Bodyguard strategy was like a successful lie: it had just enough truth to make it seem plausible.

Diplomacy – the conduct of relations between governments.

EYEWITNESS: Irwin Rommel, commander, Army Group B, January 1944

"If we cannot get at the enemy immediately after he lands, we will never be able to make another move, because of his vastly superior air forces. If we are not able to repulse the enemy at sea or throw him off the mainland in the first 48 hours, then the invasion will have succeeded and the war will be lost."

U.S. B-17 Flying Fortresses head toward targets in Germany.

JANUARY 1, France
Hitler agrees to von Rundstedt's proposal that Rommel should command a new army group to be known as Army Group B. The new unit will be subordinate to von Rundstedt's OB West.

JANUARY 2, London
Montgomery arrives in London to take up his post. Eisenhower visits Washington, D.C., before he also flies to London.

JANUARY 3, London
Montgomery chairs his first Overland planning conference. He tells his staff he thinks the proposed three-division assault from three bridgeheads is too narrow and will fail.

Rommel tours beach defenses in France in early 1944.

JANUARY 4, Devon, Britain
American troops undertake their first major amphibious training exercise.

JANUARY 7, France
General Alfred Jodl, chief of operations for the German Army High Command, begins a tour to assess the readiness of the German defenses along the English Channel.

OB West – the command of all German forces in western Europe.

Hundreds of M4 Sherman tanks are stored ready for the invasion.

JANUARY 11, Great Britain
The U.S. 4th Armored Division is the first U.S. armored unit to arrive in Britain.

JANUARY 11, Germany
The U.S. Eighth Army Air Force bombs German fighter production plants.

JANUARY 13, France
General Alfred Jodl visits Cherbourg and finds its defenses in a state of chaos. He orders Cherbourg and the major French ports to be fortified ready to face an invasion.

JANUARY 17, London
Eisenhower appoints General Omar N. Bradley as future commanding officer of all U.S. armies in the field.

JANUARY 19, France
The French Resistance requests an increase in the arms and supplies it receives from the Allies.

JANUARY 21, France
After a secret mission, British combat swimmers report firm sand and few obstacles on the landing beaches.

JANUARY 22, Italy
The Allies make the last large-scale seaborne attack on German territory before Operation Overlord when they attack Anzio, south of Rome.

JANUARY 26, Great Britain
Eisenhower tells General Patton that Patton will command the U.S. Third Army for its breakout from the Normandy bridgehead.

JANUARY 27, France
All cross-Channel raiding by the Allies is halted ahead of the invasion.

JANUARY 31, Great Britain
There are now almost one million U.S. troops in Great Britain. This figure will double over the next 12 weeks.

Allied landing craft are prepared for the invasion.

Bridgehead – a small foothold of land occupied in enemy territory.

EYEWITNESS: Edgar Feuchtinger, 21st Panzer Division, Caen

"Our division is the only one near the coast behind the Atlantic Wall, which, here in Normandy, is not fully developed and manned by an inexperienced infantry division. We have to reckon on airborne landings or large-scale commando operations, which would serve as a diversion from the actual landings."

British troops practice overcoming a barbed wire obstacle using a ladder.

JANUARY 31, France
Rommel begins strengthening the French coastal defenses against attack.

FEBRUARY 1, London
Supreme Headquarters Allied Expeditionary Force (SHAEF) issues the Initial Joint Plan (IJP) for Operation Neptune, the naval part of Overlord, following its approval by the Combined Chiefs of Staff.

FEBRUARY 3, Great Britain
The U.S. Navy now has at least 18 major bases in Great Britain.

FEBRUARY 9, London
Britain's Home Defence Committee discusses sealing off the southern coast of England prior to Overlord. Eisenhower approves a proposal to bomb the French railroad system to prevent the Germans moving troops easily.

FEBRUARY 10, Great Britain
All landing craft no longer being used are to be returned to Great Britain from all other theaters.

FEBRUARY 11, Great Britain
The invasion force builds.

FEBRUARY 14, Great Britain
The U.S. 82nd Airborne Division arrives in England from Sicily.

STRATEGY AND TACTICS: Visitor ban

Prime Minister Winston Churchill initially rejected the idea of blocking off England's south coast from public access because he thought it would be unpopular. However, he was willing to change his mind on security grounds. He asked for a written list—on one sheet of paper—of things that the public should not see. The list revealed there were few locations between Suffolk and Cornwall that would not be involved in Neptune and Overlord. Churchill gave his agreement to the plan.

Landing craft – flat-bottomed boats for landing troops and supplies on beaches.

German troops were sent to Russia in early 1944 as a result of Allied deception.

FEBRUARY 16, France
Grand Admiral Karl Dönitz orders the transfer of 10 submarines from the French coast to Norway.

FEBRUARY 18, London
The Luftwaffe begins the "Little Blitz," a series of bombing raids that kill 961 Londoners and injure more than 1700.

FEBRUARY 19, Great Britain
Exercise Crackshot begins; this is a large-scale exercise for medical troops and hospitals in southern England to assess the best way to deal with high numbers of wounded.

FEBRUARY 28, France
Adolf Hitler continues to move troops from the West to shore up his collapsing Eastern Front.

FEBRUARY 28–29, Great Britain
In London, the Home Defence Committee recommends new security measures to guard the secrecy of Overlord. The British government imposes a press ban to stop newspapers from speculating about the timing, location, and size of the invasion, even though many commentators are aware that an invasion must eventually come.

MARCH 1, Great Britain
The Home Defence Committee endorses banning visitors from the south coast, and

STRATEGY AND TACTICS: Initial Joint Plan

The Allied Initial Joint Plan (IJP) for D-Day called for five landings along the French coast between the Cotentin Peninsula in the east and the estuary of the Orne River in the west. The five assault beaches were codenamed Utah, Omaha, Gold, Juno, and Sword. Reinforcements, totalling 20 divisions, were to be in France by D+20. The U.S. First Army would take charge of the Utah and Omaha landings. Its task would be cut off the peninsula and protect the rear of the division attacking Cherbourg. British and Canadian units of the British Second Army would assault Gold, Juno, and Sword, the three eastern beaches. The division from Sword would capture Caen. The invasion front would be protected by airborne troops. The IJP assumed that the assault divisions could breach the German coastal defenses, organize its troops, and advance inland over 12 miles (19 km) in one day. As events proved, the plan was over ambitious.

Blitz – a sustained bombing campaign against a target.

suggests extending the ban to other coasts. Churchill is reluctant to adopt the measure. He holds the first weekly meeting of the Overlord Preparation Committee.

U.S. paratroopers prepare for a training flight in southern England.

MARCH 6, France

RAF Bomber Command bombs rail targets to test the effectiveness of the Zuckerman Transportation Plan, which recommends bombing the German-controlled French railroads. The raids involve saturation bombing of small targets at night. Raids continue for three weeks.

MARCH 10, France

Rommel's Army Group B moves to a castle northwest of Paris to be closer to the coast and to OB West HQ at St Germain.

MARCH 10, Great Britain

Churchill finally agrees to ban the movement of civilians from the south and east coasts.

A young German gun crew man their self-propelled antitank gun.

MARCH 19, Germany

Hitler holds a conference at his Berchtesgaden mountain retreat with his senior commanders in the West. Rommel privately asks Hitler to extend his authority at von Rundstedt's expense. Hitler suggests a compromise.

EYEWITNESS: Margaret Seeley, WRN messenger

"I remember bicycling all around Southampton and the roads were lined with American troops. They'd all sort of converged, and these huge American lorries full of GIs, and they all whistled at us and threw us Mars bars and bits of chocolate. One just waved at them and thanked them and went on our way. But the Americans were everywhere."

Saturation bombing – heavily bombing an area, rather than a specific target.

EYEWITNESS: John H. Biddle, 323rd Bomb Group, USAF

"Before D-Day we were doing 'pre-invasion' bombing. We were hitting airfields, railroad marshaling yards, transportation systems, and communications systems. Then we started on the bridges. My 49th mission was a raid against the port of Dieppe. It was one minute and thirty seconds over enemy territory. The flak was heavy, intense, and packed. The aircraft was hit, as well as the pilot, and it was out of control and the order came to bail out."

MARCH 20, Germany

Hitler issues his assessment of Allied intentions. He knows that an invasion of mainland Europe is likely, but he does not know where. He gives orders that, wherever the invasion comes, it must be quashed within hours.

MARCH 24, France

The Combined Chiefs of Staff decide that, since the invasion fleet for Operation Neptune is to have priority, the invasion of southern France will not be launched at the same time. It will be postponed until landing craft are available, delaying it until July 10 at the earliest.

MARCH 25, France

Despite his warnings about an Allied invasion, Hitler continues to strip troops from the West to send to the Eastern Front, where the German position is becoming more desperate.

A U.S. B-26 Marauder returns from a bombing mission over northern France.

MARCH 29, Great Britain

Britain's ultra-secret radio intelligence base Station X at Bletchley Park intercepts and decodes a movement order from Berlin to II SS Panzer Corps in France. Bomber Command bombs the Corps' assembly point around the rail junction at Vaires, hitting the munitions store and killing 1,200 soldiers. The Panzer division is temporarily crippled.

MARCH 31, France

The French coast is under constant Allied surveillance. Recent photographs reveal a dramatic increase in the number of German gun batteries in the Normandy assault area.

Surveillance – monitoring enemy movement and communications.

British troops wade ashore from Landing Craft, Infantry (LCI) on a training mission.

APRIL 1, Great Britain
Civilians are barred from a zone that extends 10 miles (16 km) inland from the English coast.

APRIL 2, Great Britain
Churchill agrees to a request from the Chiefs of Staff to reorganize Britain's anti-aircraft defenses to protect the invasion fleet, despite continued German air raids on British cities.

APRIL 6, France
Hitler declares that he thinks it unlikely there will be an Allied invasion. But he orders a defensive line to be set up between the Seine River and the Belgian border, and orders Normandy to be reinforced.

APRIL 7, London
Exercise Thunderclap is the largest briefing meeting for Overlord ground forces; it involves officers from all the field armies, who war-game worst-case scenarios.

APRIL 10, London
Naval HQ issues the Operation Neptune naval orders. The 1,100-page document covers every aspect of the cross-Channel operation.

STRATEGY AND TACTICS:
Operation Neptune

Admiral Sir Bertram Ramsay's orders of April 10 organized an invasion fleet of 4,126 amphibious landing craft, supported by 1,141 warships and more than 224 cargo vessels. It was split into five forces; one for each beach. Each force was made up of 16 separate convoys. There would also be two follow-up forces. All forces would converge before crossing the Channel. Minesweepers would sail south to clear five channels, with each channel having two lanes to provide a clear run for slower and faster vessels to the Normandy coast.

USS *Texas* was tasked with bombarding positions on Omaha Beach.

STRATEGY AND TACTICS:
Invasion air cover

Air Chief Marshal Sir Trafford Leigh-Mallory was responsible for air cover for the invasion fleet. His plan called for 171 squadrons during D-Day alone, including 3,700 fighter aircraft. They would provide cover over the landing beaches, support for ground troops, and escorts for bombers attacking the German coastal defenses. It was vital for the progress of the air campaign to establish airfields in Normandy as soon as possible. Three emergency landing strips and later four refuelling and rearming strips were to be established. To build these, British and U.S. engineers were formed into 23 airfield construction groups ready to head for France.

APRIL 14, Great Britain
One of the main requirements for the launch of Overlord has been met: the Allies have air superiority after the success of Operation Pointblank, the bombing of German targets.

APRIL 15, Great Britain
A crisis looms as it becomes clear that warships will have to be removed from every theater of war to cover the invasion.

APRIL 17, Great Britain
The Royal Navy starts to lay mines off the French coast in preparation for Operation Neptune. More than 6,800 mines will be laid off the Channel ports in France and Holland in an attempt to keep German surface vessels confined to port.

Rows of Bofors light antiaircraft guns await transportation to the front.

APRIL 24, Great Britain
All civilian travel overseas is now banned.

APRIL 25, Great Britain
German bombers attack Portsmouth in an attempt to disrupt invasion preparations.

APRIL 26, Great Britain
A full-scale rehearsal of Operation Neptune begins (Exercise Tiger). Britain is now effectively sealed off from the world.

APRIL 28, Great Britain
Disaster strikes Exercise Tiger. German torpedo-armed boats attack a convoy of Landing Ships, Tank (LSTs), involved in the exercise off the coast at Slapton Sands. The attack leaves 700 soldiers dead and wipes out the operational reserve of LSTs for Operation Overlord.

APRIL 29, France
German surface vessels become increasingly aggressive as they try to stop Allied vessels from laying mines close to the French shore. Churchill persuades Eisenhower to reduce the bombing of targets on French railroads in order to avoid civilian casualties.

Mines – floating bombs that detonate when they are struck by a ship.

MAY 1, Great Britain
The invasion deception directorate issues the coded message "Word is Vendetta." It sparks a wave of sabotage from Norway to the Balkans to distract the enemy.

MAY 2, Great Britain
Eisenhower sets the earliest possible date for D-Day as June 5. A British newspaper crossword contains the clue "Utah." Is this a security breach or a coincidence?

MAY 3, France
RAF Bomber Command increases raids on German military targets.

MAY 8, Great Britain
Exercise Fabius ends after two days; it has seen assault divisions practice amphibious landings in the last full-scale rehearsal before D-Day.

MAY 9, France
Rommel tours the Normandy beaches and finds them too thinly defended.

Resistance fighters in France learn how to strip a Sten gun.

MAY 10, France
Allied air raids begin to destroy the chain of German radar stations along the northern coast of France.

A train in France; the Allies tried to destroy the French rail network.

EYEWITNESS: Ewell Lunsford, Operation Tiger

"We were torpedoed by German E-boats. The whole end was knocked off the ship I was on. I was down in the hold with the vehicles and gasoline and ammunition, and just packed in there. I heard one torpedo come sliding down the side of the hull, and it didn't explode. The next one caught the stern and tore off about 30 feet (9 m) all the way across the end."

Sabotage – acts of damage that harm an enemy's war effort.

DUKW amphibious vehicles are lined up ready for action.

MAY 17, Great Britain
Eisenhower confirms D-Day will be June 5. All preparations must be complete by June 1.

MAY 22, Great Britain
Another crossword clue in *The Daily Telegraph* has the answer "Omaha." Some people think this cannot be a coincidence.

MAY 27, Great Britain
Another answer to a crossword clue in the same paper, Overlord, sends security officers to find out who is setting the puzzles. Air attacks in the Channel are halted ahead of the crossing.

MAY 28, Great Britain
The invasion fleet and troops are ready. Now they just need good weather to safely cross the English Channel.

MAY 29, Great Britain
At this late date, there are doubts about the U.S. airborne plan.

MAY 30, Great Britain
Eisenhower insists that the Utah airdrop must go ahead despite the risks.

MAY 30, Germany
Hitler is told that the expected Allied invasion is not imminent, but that when it comes it will probably come through the Pas de Calais, at the narrowest point of the Channel.

MAY 31, Great Britain
Troops, vehicles, and equipment are loaded onto the invasion fleet. More than 6,000 containers of equipment have now been dropped to the French Resistance.

KEY PEOPLE: Field Marshal Irwin Rommel

Rommel was a decorated World War I veteran whose career took off when Hitler came to power. During the 1940 invasion of France, his speedy advance to the English Channel earned him a reputation as a daring tank commander. This reputation was cemented as commander of the Afrika Korps from 1941. Rommel's victories in North Africa led to promotion to field marshal. He left North Africa in 1943, and was charged with establishing anti-invasion plans on the Channel coast. He commanded Army Group B after the Allied landings in June 1944, and was badly injured during an air attack. Implicated in the failed July 1944 plot against Adolf Hitler, he chose to kill himself.

French Resistance – a secret group fighting the German occupation in France

Landing Craft, Tank (LCTs) are loaded at an English coastal port.

JUNE 1, Great Britain

The embarkation of invasion troops continues. Admiral Ramsay assumes operational command of the invasion fleet and the English Channel. He persuades Winston Churchill and King George VI not to sail with the invasion fleet. Both of them had expressed a wish to accompany the Allied forces on D-Day.

JUNE 1, Great Britain

Eisenhower and his commanders in chief will meet morning and evening for the latest weather forecasts.

JUNE 1, Great Britain

From Bush House in central London, the BBC begins to broadcast a coded message to Resistance groups in France, warning them that the invasion is imminent. German intelligence intercepts the message but interprets it as meaning that there will be general French Resistance action against trains and the railroads. They do not connect the sabotage and the imminent Allied invasion.

German commanders study maps of the French coast.

EYEWITNESS: John Blake, Royal Army Service Corps

"We moved down to Tilbury and were put on an American Liberty ship. This meant lifting the trucks on. We just sat in the trucks and they lifted us up and put us down in the hold. We drove onto this wire netting stuff that had a hook at each end and they just hooked it on to one of the cranes on the ship and, whoosh, we were on, in no time at all."

Embarkation – loading men and equipment onto boats.

German half-tracks with anti-aircraft cannon move into position in France.

JUNE 2, Great Britain

Leigh-Mallory presents his pre-invasion bombing plan, which will target major roads into the assault area in order to slow down the movement of German reinforcements.

JUNE 2, France

Despite all the indications that the Allied invasion is about to begin, Hitler again strips OB West of mechanized units in order to support defenses elsewhere. In Italy, the U.S. VI Corps has broken out of the Anzio bridgehead and is threatening Rome from the south. Hitler orders 19 air force divisions and several tank battalions from the West to reinforce a new German defensive line north of Rome.

JUNE 3, Great Britain

The Joint Intelligence Committee makes its final report on enemy assessments of the Allied invasion plans. The report argues that there is no evidence that the enemy knows accurately where the invasion will take place. The Germans seems to expect a landing between Pas de Calais and Cherbourg. But, the report concludes, the enemy definitely expects an invasion to begin imminently.

JUNE 4, Great Britain

At 04:15 a.m., a briefing by army meteorologists in London reports that there is no sign of the weather improving. Eisenhower confirms the postponement of D-Day. The invasion will now take place on June 6, as long as the weather improves over the next 12 hours. At the 17:45 briefing, a period of settled weather is forecast

KEY PEOPLE: General Charles De Gaulle

Charles de Gaulle served in World War I as a young officer and remained in the French Army until June 1940, when the Germans took France. Escaping to England, he denounced the Vichy Regime for collaborating with the Germans, and called on the French to fight against the German occupiers. In exile, he became the figurehead of the French Resistance, but other Allied leaders found him difficult to work with. De Gaulle was only told of the plan for D-Day just before the invasion, and was furious about being left in the dark. He maneuvered to make sure that his Free French movement played a key role in the liberation of Paris. Following the Allied victory, De Gaulle became president of France and was a key figure in French politics until his death in 1970.

Meteorologist – a scientist who studies and predicts weather patterns.

Allied troops on board a landing craft are finally told their destination.

from Monday evening until dawn on the Tuesday. This is the most promising forecast for the next three days, but it is far short of the lengthy spell of good weather the invasion commanders had been hoping for.

JUNE 4, France

A German Air Force meteorologist in Paris advises that due to expected bad weather in the Channel the Allied invasion will not be able to take place for at least two weeks.

JUNE 4, France

Bomber raids on German coastal defenses in France are stepped up for the last push before D-Day. In the last four days, the U.S. Eighth Army Air Force has made 2,200 bomber sorties.

JUNE 5, Great Britain

At a briefing at invasion headquarters in London at 04:15 a.m., it is confirmed that the weather reports have been accurate and that the period of fair weather will last until late on Tuesday. The Supreme Commander confirms that the invasion will proceed at dawn on June 6. The invasion fleet sets sail. As the invasion fleet begins to assemble south of the Isle of Wight ready to cross the Channel, it is given air cover from fighters from 16:00 hours.

EYEWITNESS: Eisenhower's Order of the Day, June 5

"Soldiers, Sailors, and Airmen of the Allied Expeditionary Force! You are about to embark upon a great crusade, toward which we have striven these many months. The eyes of the world are upon you...
I have full confidence in your courage, devotion to duty, and skill in battle. We will accept nothing less than full victory! Good Luck!"

U.S. paratroopers board a C-47 transport plane to fly to France.

Paratrooper – a soldier who parachutes into battle.

German infantry move into position near the Orne River.

JUNE 5, Great Britain
The first U.S. airborne troops take off from Berkshire at about 21:50 hours. Loaded into C-47 transports, they are the pathfinder teams of the 101st Airborne. They are to land 30 minutes ahead of the main paratroopers, to identify and mark drop zones (DZ) with flares and radio direction sets. Between 22:33 and 23:07 hours, three RAF bombers take off to parachute men into the Brittany area so they can make contact with Resistance groups.

JUNE 5, France
Rommel draws up a situation report for von Rundstedt at OB West, stating that bad weather means there is no imminent danger of invasion. The Seventh Army commander, General Dollman, orders a relaxation of the standing alert along the French coast. He summons senior officers to attend a war game exercise in Rennes, 125 miles (200 km) from the landing sites in Normandy.

JUNE 5, Normandy
The first German units to face the coming Allied invasion will be the six infantry and three panzer divisions now settling down for the night in Normandy. They are concentrated in the Cotentin Peninsula, protecting the port of Cherbourg, and along the Calvados Coast, from the River Vire in the west to the River Dives, 10 miles (16 km) east of Caen. The divisions vary widely in their equipment, the experience of their personnel, and their fighting ability.

STRATEGY AND TACTICS: The landing beaches
As laid down in Appendix VIII (Annex B) of the voluminous orders for Operation Neptune, the D-Day assault area covered a distance of 61.7 miles (98.7 km) along the Calvados Coast of the Bay of Seine. The coast was divided up into the five assault areas that have gone down in history as the five D-Day beaches: Utah, Omaha, Gold, Juno, and Sword. In fact, the landing objectives were not identified in this way. To make navigation more precise, the orders divided the five areas into sectors that were identified phonetically, as Able, Baker, Charlie, and so on. The sectors were subdivided into assault beaches, codenamed White, Green, and Red. In this way, the landings on Gold, for example, were to be made over Jig Green, Jig Red, King Green, and King Red.

Pathfinder – a soldier who marks a landing zone or other path.

The invasion fleet begins to assemble before crossing the English Channel.

EYEWITNESS: Major John Howard, Caen Canal

"The glider suddenly did a right-hand turn, and then another right-hand turn, so that we were coming into the landing zone from the south, losing height all the way. I could see the River Orne and the Caen Canal, reflected in the half-moon. And we came to what we knew was going to be the toughest moment of the lot: the crash land."

00:16 hours, British Sector, Normandy

Six gliders carrying Major Howard's troops on their way to seize the bridges across the Orne River and Caen Canal cross the Normandy coast. No. 1 glider crash-lands on the east bank of the canal. It plows through a belt of barbed wire before coming to a halt close to the bridge. Gliders 2 and 3 land directly behind it at one minute intervals.

00:50 hours, British Sector

The lead aircraft carrying the 5th Parachute Brigade and forward units of Lieutenant-Colonel Otway's Merville attack force fly in at a height of little more than 400 feet (120 m).

00:30 hours, Cotentin Peninsula

Transports are now flying over the peninsula between the Orne and Dives rivers to drop paratroopers who will act as pathfinders for the three Allied airborne divisions. The pathfinders are supposed to mark the drop zone (DZ) for the first airborne troops following just 30 minutes behind them. But the mission goes wrong. The peninsula is covered in cloud, and only one of the 18 U.S. pathfinder teams land in the correct place.

British glider-borne troops laugh at messages scrawled on their airplane.

Glider – An aircraft with no engine that travels on air currents.

Gliders like these made the perilous journey under the cover of darkness.

01:00 hours, English Channel

A large number of deception schemes and electronic warfare operations are in place over the English Channel and the Normandy coast to mask the invasion fleet and draw the Germans away from the airborne DZs. For the past 24 hours bombers filled with anti-radar equipment have been flying over the Channel, jamming enemy ground radar and interrupting radio frequencies.

01:00 hours, German Defenses

Allied airborne troops have been landing for nearly an hour before German troops try to organize a response. The German Navy reacts first. At 01:30 hours, Vice-Admiral Rieve, commander of the Channel coast, informs Admiral Kranke's HQ in Paris of the American landings. Kranke puts Navy Group West on alert in preparation for action.

01:30 hours, British Sector

As German Army commanders attempt to make sense of what is going on in Normandy, units of the 716th Division begin the first counter-attack on Major Howard's men at the Orne Canal.

EYEWITNESS: Major John Howard, Caen Canal

"Above all, and this was the tremendous thing, there was no firing at all. We had complete surprise: we really caught old Jerry with his pants down. I followed the platoon up the track. I saw the smoke bomb explode, the phosphorus bomb; I heard the 'thud, thud, thud' in the pillbox as the grenades exploded, and I knew we'd get no trouble from there."

British paratroopers guard a road outside the town of Ranville.

Radar – a system for locating objects by bouncing radio waves off them.

KEY WEAPONS: Beach obstacles

In anticipation of an eventual Allied invasion, the Germans had made great efforts to prepare effective defenses against an amphibious assault along potential landing areas in northern France. In addition to the Atlantic Wall fortifications, Rommel ordered the construction of a range of beach obstacles to prevent and hinder Allied landing attempts. These included iron girder constructions designed to rip the bottoms off landing craft, wooden stakes, cross-shaped obstacles known as "Czech hedgehogs," and other treacherous designs. Many of these obstacles were made more deadly with the addition of mines and explosives. The obstacles were quite successful, causing significant casualties and giving Allied commanders another problem to solve.

01:40 hours, Britain

Some 72 gliders are towed into the air carrying reinforcements and heavy equipment. In France, engineers clear landing strips for their arrival.

Troops unload supplies from a crash-landed glider.

02:00 hours, Mines

Flotillas of minesweepers and their destroyer escorts begin to arrive off the Normandy coast, exactly on schedule. Minesweepers begin clearing offshore areas prior to the arrival of the five assault forces. This work must be done in the next three hours, before the tide turns at low water at about 05:00 hours.

02:40 hours, Germany

Von Rundstedt's staff inform Rommel's chief of staff that from the information he has received, the field marshal does not consider the invasion to be a major operation.

03.00 hours, English Channel

German radar stations along the coast finally discover the Allied invasion fleet. Admiral Kranke orders his fleet to sortie from Le Havre.

03:14 hours, French Coast

As part of the pre-assault bombardment, RAF bombers begin a 75-minute bombardment of German troop concentrations along the invasion coast.

03:54–04:10 hours, U.S. Sector

Gliders carrying reinforcements and heavy equipment for the 101st and 82nd Airborne divisions begin to land. The paratroopers start to assemble in groups of no more than 10 men.

Minesweepers – small warships whose job is to locate and destroy mines.

04:15 hours, British Sector

Colonel Otway launches his attack on the Merville battery despite the fact that gliders intended to have landed paratroopers inside the battery perimeter have failed to arrive. Despite heavy casualities, the British capture the battery within 25 minutes.

American landing craft stream toward shore after the first assault wave.

05:00 hours, U.S. Sector

After a chaotic drop and several hours wandering in the dark, U.S. paratroopers begin to fight in a series of small actions. They ambush German patrols, clear villages, and establish roadblocks. As dawn approaches, men of the 101st Airborne are moving into position to hold the road exits from Utah Beach.

05:00 hours, Juno and Sword

Two Royal Navy midget submarines finally surface after spending 72 hours submerged off the invasion beaches. X-20 takes up station off Juno, while X-23 lies off Sword. Their green flashing lights will guide the invasion fleet into position off the two beaches, which are otherwise flat and featureless.

05:00 hours, French Coast

Faced with what is now clearly a major Allied landing, U-boats of Group "Landwirt" (Farmer) are ordered from French ports into the Channel. A total of 36 boats set off.

TURNING POINTS: How the world learned of D-Day

It was the Nazi regime that told the world about D-Day; and U.S. newspapers first published the news. The Nazi propaganda minister, Joseph Goebbels, had news of the invasion transmitted via his TransOcean News Agency at 07.00 hours. In the United States, Associated Press—seven hours behind Berlin—picked up the story. The *New York Times* had a special edition on the streets just 90 minutes after the Omaha landing began. In Britain, where news was tightly controlled, the public learned of D-Day at 09.30 hours, when the BBC broadcast SHAEF's "Communique No 1." This read "Allied naval forces, supported by strong air forces, began landing Allied armies this morning on the coast of northern France." Journalists were confined to the Ministry of Information building and had to submit their stories for censoring before publication.

Perimeter – a barrier around the outside of a piece of land.

EYEWITNESS: Marie-Louise Osmant, Normandy

"We see the first damage. Roof on the outbuildings heavily damaged, a heap of broken roof tiles on the ground, a few windowpanes at my place. Hundreds of slates blown off the chateau, walls cracked, shutters won't close. But at Bernice's it's worse. An airplane or tank shell has exploded on the paving in her kitchen, and the whole interior of the room is devastated."

05:36 HOURS, Utah Beach

The Allied naval bombardment of the Normandy coast begins ahead of schedule to counter German gunfire. The German coastal batteries have been unable to fire at the Allied fleet so far because the Allies have jammed their radar, but with first light they are finally able to locate targets among the warships and minesweepers offshore.

The USS *Nevada* provides gunfire support for U.S. troops at Utah Beach.

Dozens of Allied gliders lie abandoned after landing in France.

06:30–07:45 HOURS, Normandy

This short period—just one and a quarter hours—marks the H-Hours, the time for the beach assaults. Months of planning and training have come down to this brief window when the tide favors the invasion forces. Allied seaborne forces attempt to get a toehold in Nazi-occupied northern Europe, and to link up with the airborne troops scattered in Normandy. The landings will make it clear to Hitler's generals that this is, indeed, a full-scale invasion.

07:30 HOURS, British Sector

As the British 3rd Division begins to land on Sword, the 6th Airborne Division is holding the Allied left flank with five battalions centered on the canal and river bridges of the Orne. Although units of the 3rd Division are due to reach the Orne two hours after H-Hour, there is no sign of them by 09:00 hours. Meanwhile German acitivity is increasing everywhere, with constant sniping at the bridges. Commandos from the beaches finally make contact at about 13:30 hours, but the link remains weak.

Flank – the exposed side of a military formation.

05:30 hours

At 05:30 hours, the first waves of landing craft from Task Force U are on their way toward beaches Uncle Red and Tare Green, which together form a front about 2,200 yards (2,010 m) wide. The waves of landing craft are still several thousand feet from the beach when the landing schedule starts to break down. A strong tidal current is pushing the landing force off course. Meanwhile, the beach is hidden in dust and smoke from the bombardment. The LCC (Landing Craft, Control) identify the wrong stretch of coast, and the assault craft set off to land 1,500 yards (1,370 m) south of the intended arrival point.

H-HOUR: 06:30 hours

At 06:30 hours the U.S. 8th Infantry hits Utah beach. They are exactly on schedule, but by now they are 2,000 yards (1,830 m) from where they should be, having been pushed further south by the tide. In fact, this turns out to be a lucky accident: this stretch of beach is less heavily defended, and the companies make it ashore almost unopposed.

U.S. troops wade through surf to Utah Beach.

10:45 hours

The assault battalions begin to move inland in order to link up with the paratroopers they hope have secured the exits and to secure the roads leading from the beachhead.

11:10 hours

The first contact is made between U.S. seaborne forces and the paratroopers when the 2nd Battalion crosses the Exit 1 causeway and links up with men from the 501st Regiment, 101st Airborne Division,

KEY WEAPONS: The Landing Ship, Tank (LST)

The LST was vital to the success of the invasion thanks to its size and adaptability. The LST was an adapted oil tanker that had its bow cut away and replaced with hinged bow doors and long, folding ramps. The idea was that the vessel could sail virtually onto the beach so that vehicles could be driven on and off. That got rid of the need for docks and cranes. The LST was 372 feet (100 m) long and 540 feet (165 m) wide, and it could carry up to 40 Sherman tanks, or 26 vehicles and 200 troops. Its role in the invasion was not limited to shipping vehicles and men. Some LSTs were used as hospital ships, and others were used to tow parts of the Mulberry harbors into place.

Causeway – a raised embankment carrying a road.

A mobile signaling battery sets up its equipment on Utah Beach.

EYEWITNESS: Herbert Male, LCT crew, U.S. Assault Engineers

"We went into Utah about twenty minutes after H-Hour. We saw not one German aircraft over the beaches all the time I was over there. There were lots of mines on the beaches and obstructions that had to be got through. We weren't bothered at all. We had a free run into the beach. Everything went not bad at all."

east of Pouppeville. The village has been under attack from U.S. paratroopers since 08:00 hours and is now largely in U.S. hands. While the 8th Infantry move in to secure the village, the paratroopers move east toward the village of Ste Marie-du-Mont. The 8th Infantry's 3rd and 1st battalions are moving inland to secure the causeways to Exits 2 and 3.

LATE MORNING

By now there is serious congestion at the Utah beachhead. None of the exits from the beach has been entirely secured, and Allied vehicles are beginning to back up along the beach roads. This causes special problems for the beach controllers, who are tasked with supervising the movement of the assault forces off the beach. The commanders of the 12th and 22nd Infantry regiments, which are a long way south of where they should be, are in danger of missing their D-Day objectives altogether without decisive action. They decide to march their battalions off the roads across countryside that has been deliberately flooded by the Germans. They head toward the higher ground around the village of Ste Martin-de-Varreville, which is supposed to be in the hands of the 101st Airborne. Wading through water up chest deep, the march takes nearly four hours to cover just little over 1 mile (1.6 km).

Wrecked U.S. hardware lies littered on Utah Beach.

Congestion – blockages that cause delay.

STRATEGY AND TACTICS: The U.S. Airborne

The 82nd and 101st Airborne Divisions of the U.S. Army played a vital role in the D-Day landings on June 6. The 82nd was the first airborne division of the army. Before Normandy, it had played a key role in the invasions of Sicily and Italy, where it refined its tactics for an aerial assault. The 101st ("Screaming Eagles") saw action on Utah Beach before playing a pivotal role in the later engagements of the war. Their task on D-Day was to land behind Utah Beach and take out the Germans' secondary beach defenses. The drop went wrong, and 1,500 soldiers missed the landing zones and were either killed or captured. Despite this, the survivors persevered to complete their mission.

22:30 hours

By dusk, the 12th Infantry has made a rapid advance and is over 5 miles (8 km) inland, preparing to move north. The right flank of the Allied invasion front is now being held by seven battalions of infantry. The 22nd Infantry now holds the village of St Germain de Varreville with two battalions and moves a third along the beach road to a position 4 miles (6 km) north of the assault beaches.

24:00 hours

The 8th Infantry, having access to the roads leading from Exits 1, 2, and 3, and supported by tanks, are over 6 miles (9 km) inland. The 2nd Battalion has moved through Ste Marie du Mont and made contact with the 3rd Battalion from Exit 2 to the north. They have seized the crossroads of the main Carentan-Cherbourg road at Les Forges. They are only 2 miles (3 km) south of their goal of Ste Mere Eglise, but they now face a large pocket of German resistance before they can relieve the paratroopers who are holding the village. Facing the Germans to the east is the 1st Battalion, which has advanced up the road from Exit 3 through the hamlet of Andouville la Hubert.

A U.S. battleship pounds enemy positions as an LCT heads for the beach.

24:00 hours, Assessment

The D-Day landings on Utah beach can be said to be a qualified success. Over 20,000 troops have been landed, with 1,700 vehicles. But, the Utah bridgehead remains very small and the advance is nearly 7 miles (11 km) short of its objective.

AIRBORNE ASSAULT
09:30 hours

After a chaotic series of drops and landings, the American airborne divisions hold only some of their D-Day objectives. They face superior numbers of German

Relieve – to come to the aid of a unit that is under attack

U.S. troops make their way inland through flooded fields.

forces. Fortunately, the disorganized assault has confused the Germans, who are staying in their fixed positions and not counterattacking. They do not know how many paratroopers they face and what their objectives are.

09:30 hours

Three hours after the landings on Utah beach began, the Germans launch a counterattack south of Ste Mere Eglise in an attempt to retake the village captured at dawn by the 82nd Airborne's 505th Regiment. The 2nd Battalion to the north, at Neuville au Plain, is pulled back to defend the village, but leaves only 42 paratroopers to defend Neuville. They hold off the German 1058th Regiment for eight hours, but only 16 of the 42 paratroopers survives the fight. Meanwhile a company size counterattack by paratroopers on a German convoy on the Caretan road secures Ste Mère Eglise for the rest of the day.

24:00 hours, Causeway

The sucess of the U.S. airborne divisions hides the fact that they are understrength. Of more than 12,000 paratroopers who boarded airplanes in England, barely 5,000 are organized and facing the enemy by the end of D-Day. The rest are scattered, lost, or dead.

Troops, vehicles, and equipment pour into the beachhead.

EYEWITNESS: Tom Treanor, war correspondent, Utah Beach

"The general lack of fortifications was astonishing. The barbed wire consisted of four single strands such as we use at home to fence in cattle. The engineers had blown gaps in the wire through which we could move vehicles. A few dead lay about and some wounded were here and there on stretchers awaiting transport to ships out at sea. All up and down the beach as far as I could see, men, jeeps, bulldozers and other equipment were moving about like ants."

Counterattack – an attack launched in response to an enemy attack.

05:50 hours

At Omaha Beach, the naval bombardment begins on schedule. But almost immediately the invasion plan starts to go wrong. The air bombardment, due to strike at 06:00 hours, does not materialize. For the assault to work, overwhelming firepower to break the coastal defences is needed. This will allow the first wave of infantry to land largely unopposed. But, 500 bombers of the Eighth Army Air Force miss the coast completely because of low cloud. They drop 1,200 tons (1,220 tonnes) of bombs on positions 3 miles (5 km) inland. At sea, meanwhile, the DD tanks are sinking. Launched 5,000 yards (4,575 m) offshore at 05:40 hours, no consideration has been made for rough seas. A swell swamps 27 of 32 first-wave tanks. The rough seas are also pulling the assault craft out of position. As they approach the beach at 06:30 hours, most of them are over 1,000 yards (900 m) east of their destination.

U.S. troops head for the coast under heavy German machine-gun fire.

06:30 hours; H-Hour

As the landing craft approach the beach at H-Hour, the Germans hold their fire. As the craft near the beaches and their ramps are lowered, every German gun on Omaha opens fire on the U.S. troops. It is a slaughter. Many soldiers jump from their landing craft in deep water and are drowned when their heavy equipment pulls them under.

06:40 hours

Within minutes of the start of the invasion, the command structure of

STRATEGY AND TACTICS: Beach defenses at Omaha

German commanders had identified Omaha beach as a potential landing site. From April 1944 they had turned it into a virtually impregnable defensive position. There were three belts of anti-landing obstacles on the beach, and a triple belt of barbed wire and mines along the sea wall. Beyond the beach road, the Germans dug an anti-tank ditch and bunkers. They blocked the beach road with a concrete barrier 12 feet (3.6 m) thick. The bluffs above were defended with mines, barbed wire, and trip-wired explosives. The most powerful defenses were concentrated above the beach. Eight concrete strongpoints were each manned by 30 men, equipped with machine guns, mortars, rocket launchers, and artillery pieces. Behind the strongpoints were a further 800 men of the 352nd Division who had trained for three months to face an invasion force.

DD tanks – duplex drive tanks, adapted to "swim" in water.

the assault companies has begun to collapse. Company A of the 116th Regiment is the only company in the first wave to land in the right place, but has lost all its sergeants and all but one of its officers in just 10 minutes. Elsewhere, waterlogged men leaving the sea struggle under fire across 300 yards (275 m) of open beach to take cover under a shingle bank. Others come ashore only to find themselves lost and out of sight of the beach exits.

A U.S. machine-gun crew provides covering fire for their comrades.

As the first assault wave dies on the beach, the follow-on waves of troops and equipment keep coming. Radio contact has been lost with the lead companies, and without news that the first wave has failed, the invasion schedule carries on as planned.

08:30 hours

Not a single man or vehicle has moved off the beach. The plan to take Omaha has collapsed and the invasion is in danger of failing. Despite a signal being sent out to suspend further landings, follow-up units are still coming in. Offshore, word is finally getting to the

U.S. assault troops keep their heads down as they approach the beach.

EYEWITNESS: Herbert Krieger, 29th Infantry Division

"When I landed on the beach it was covered with bodies. Most were not covered and some had boxes over them while others looked to be covered with Indian blankets, which I thought to be strange. Still others were in pieces. At about that time we were all separated."

Shingle – a beach made up of gravel and small pebbles.

generals that the landings are in deep trouble. General Bradley considers abandoning Omaha altogether and ordering Task Force O to land with the British on Gold Beach.

Meanwhile, three companies of the 2nd Rangers successfully scale the cliffs at Pointe du Hoc and surprise the German soldiers who had believed the cliffs unassailable from the sea.

U.S. Army Rangers show how they scaled the Pointe du Hoc.

08:30 hours

As the Omaha plan falls apart, the infantry, pinned down under enemy fire, begin to advance off the beach. To begin with, this is simply an attempt to survive. Colonel George Taylor tells his 16th Infantry, "There are two types of people on this beach: those who are dead and those who are about to die. So let's get the hell out of here!" Organization starts to reassert itself and the troops start to make some headway in small groups, often led by an NCO or junior officer. To the senior officers on the command ships stationed several miles out, the situation still looks bad. But the men on the beach are making slow, but steady progress. They make it to the top of the Les Moulins draw, or gully, heading toward St Laurent.

09:50 hours

General Clarence Huebner, commander of the 1st Division, receives a message saying, "There are too many vehicles on the beach. Send combat troops." It is the first optimistic sign of the morning. Huebner sends in the 18th and 115th infantry regiments to land on Easy Red, the central sector of the beach.

TURNING POINTS: Pointe du Hoc

Pointe du Hoc is a stretch of 100-foot (33-m) high cliffs on the Normandy coast between Utah beach to the west and Omaha beach to the east. The Germans placed 650mm cannons on the headland that could target both beaches and they fortified the cliff top from any Allied attack. As fighting began on Omaha, three companies of the 2nd Rangers made a daring assault on the position. They scaled the cliffs using portable ladders and attacked the six huge concrete gun emplacements, meeting little resistance. German reinforcements soon arrived, but the Rangers held the position at Pointe du Hoc until they were relieved by forces from the beaches the following day.

NCO– non-commissioned officer; a junior officer promoted from the ranks.

11.00 hours
Observers report "Men advancing up slope behind Easy Red." By midday, U.S. forces are on the plateau above the beach and are moving inland. The beach remains under heavy fire, however.

Men of the U.S. 2nd Infantry Division make their way inland from Omaha.

13:00 hours
The draw, or pass, toward St Laurent is opened to vehicles. In the afternoon, U.S. forces attack villages above the beach.

17:00 hours
The pass carrying the beach road to Vierville falls into U.S. hands when engineers blow up the concrete roadblock.

24:00 hours
More than 4,000 men have been killed. Those who have made it ashore hold a line only 1 mile (1.6 km) from the beach, with little more than their personal weapons to defend it. Only about 5 percent of the supplies have landed. In spite of this, the fight at Omaha has broken the front-line strength of the Germans and a counterattack fails to materialize.

U.S. soldiers stand guard over captured German prisoners.

EYEWITNESS: "Knobby" Walsh, 2nd Ranger Battalion

"I looked behind me and the tide was coming over the edge of that hole like Niagara Falls. I had to get out and forward. As I ran forward I could see bullets shooting up the small pebbles. The next thing I knew I was hit in the head like a blow from a baseball bat. My helmet was cast away and my neck was bleeding fast."

Plateau – a raised area of flat land.

British troops pour ashore on Gold Beach on D-Day.

07:25 hours

The assault sectors of Gold are over 3 miles (5 km) wide, and large enough to land four battalions in two brigades, side by side. On either side are well defended villages with strongpoints and emplacements which look onto the beach. But the coast between is only defended at certain points, and the beach is flat, making it ideal for an assault landing. The current and strong winds are causing problems on Gold. The infantry assault waves come in on time, but the current pulls the 231st Brigade hundreds of feet to the east of its intended position and it lands on Jig Red.

The 1st Hampshire Battalion is pushed further down the coast. Instead of landing at Le Hamel it is forced to fight a German strongpoint before it advances to and takes Le Hamel. The village is not secured until 20:00 hours.

09:50 hours

The landing beaches are secure, and follow-up units and armor begin to land.

11:00 hours

Two more brigades begin landing, to take up a position between the two initial assault brigades. During the day, getting tanks over the landing beaches proves difficult. More than 100 vehicles become bogged down in the clay and are then swamped by the rising tide. But the 151st Brigade has at least three battalions in action by D-Day afternoon.

16.00 hours

A German battle group of the 352nd Division from Bayeux—two infantry battalions supported by an anti-tank battalion—launches a counterattack on the 69th Brigade near Bazenville. The attack is beaten off with heavy German losses. By the end of the

EYEWITNESS: Leslie Gibson, private, 6th Battalion, Border Regiment

"There was everything flying about. There were these cross-girders with mines on the top and the first chap I saw was a rubber-suited frogman, minus a leg, lying on the beach. Of course there was lots of other debris. We were very lucky because we did have a shell ricochet under the boat."

Frogman – a combat swimmer with a wetsuit and breathing apparatus.

A Royal Marine commando fires his Bren light machine gun.

day the 69th Brigade is within 2 miles (3 km) of Ste Léger and the Caen-Bayeux road.

LATE AFTERNOON

The 1st Hampshire Regiment has arrived at the outskirts of Arromanches, having met no German counterattack. It bypasses the town to secure a nearby gun battery, then enters Arromanches, where the German garrison surrenders. Along the rest of the front, other brigades have stopped short of their targets but overall the day has gone well. Cheering French civilians greet the British troops with flowers, waving British and French flags.

24:00 hours

The British 56th and 151st Brigades remain short of their D-Day objectives, at least partly through a seeming lack of urgency. Nevertheless, the Gold lodgement area covers 5 square miles (13 sq km), and the whole of the 50th Division—nearly 25,000 men—are ashore. The division's right has been secured with the arrival of the 7th Canadian Brigade from Juno Beach, but the left flank is still open, and there is no sign of the U.S. forces who are tasked wth guarding it. Losses in some battalions have been heavy. The 1st Hampshire Regiment has suffered 270 casualties out of the 700 men who landed.

British infantry and commandos file past military vehicles on the beach.

STRATEGY AND TACTICS: The Canadians

Over the course of the war, 1.1 million Canadians and Newfoundlanders from a population of 11 million served as part of the Commonwealth forces. On D-Day, the Canadians had responsibility for Juno Beach. Within the first hour of landing, the 3rd Canadian Division had suffered heavy casualties. By the end of D-Day, the Canadians had penetrated further into France than any of the Allies. In the first six days of the invasion, around 3,000 Canadians were killed or wounded. But the infantry fought on, moving inland to capture enemy targets throughout June and July.

Garrison – a military unit defending a town or strongpoint.

07:35 hours

As with Gold Beach, the Juno assault sectors are wide enough to allow a two-brigade front of 6 miles (10 km). The German defenses, manned by units of the 716th Infantry Division, are concentrated in the towns, farms, and villages dotted across the flat landscape. The beaches are defended with minefields, anti-tank ditches, and the occasional bunker.

To break through this thinly held defensive line, the British I Corps is relying on the specialist equipment of the 79th Armoured Division. Each unit carries three teams of the innovative tanks known as "Hobart's Funnies" to smash through the beach road.

07:45 hours

Conditions at sea and rocks spoil the landing plan. H-Hour for the 8th Brigade is delayed by 10 minutes to 07:45 hours. The delay means that the landing craft are now heading toward beach obstacles that are being hidden by the tide; engineers will not have enough time to clear paths through them before the arrival of follow-on assault waves.

The British battleship HMS *Rodney* pounds enemy positions on shore.

08:00 hours

Despite the difficulties, the Canadian infantry secure Juno in a series of actions. In the first hours, they will clear a number of villages in house-to-house fighting.

08:30 hours

The rising tide and uncleared beach obstacles create serious congestion in one of the landing sectors. One regiment lands now but is still on the beach at 14:00 hours. The follow-up brigade does not begin to land until 10:50 hours and does not move until 16:00 hours, too late to secure its D-Day objective.

Canadian troops come ashore at Juno Beach from a range of landing craft.

12:00 hours

There is some progress around Bernieres. By noon, the first self-propelled artillery regiments are ashore, and in action.

13:00 hours

The division commander, Major-General Keller, lands and establishes his HQ. The Canadians are supposed to secure Ste Aubin before the commandos land at

Bunker – a buried, heavily reinforced defensive position.

Men of the 13/18th Hussars get a chance to rest and eat in France.

the east end of the village. However, the pre-landing bombardment has completely missed Ste Aubin, and German defenses are still intact when the Canadians arrive. The North Shore Regiment is still fighting house-to-house as commandos begin to land. The commandos are pinned down under a sea wall and take most of the day getting off the beach. They secure the area by nightfall, with the help of the Canadian armor. But losses are severe, with over 100 dead. Patrols return from Lion-sur-Mer with news that the coast east toward Sword is still in German hands.

EYEWITNESS: Frederick Jenkins, Royal Berkshires

"You can't imagine how many ships were there. You couldn't have got any more in. The corvettes, the destroyers, the Landing Ship Rockets were all starting their bombardment, and the bombardment was colossal. The whole seashore looked like a blue haze, there were smoke shells bursting to cover the landing, and it looked pretty hectic."

17:00 hours

The Canadian advance from Juno slows down as the day goes on. This is due to congestion on the beach, and German resistance. To the west, the Winnipeg Rifles are consolidating positions around Creully and have made contact with the British from Gold Beach.

KEY WEAPONS: Hobart's "Funnies"

Named for Major-General Percy Hobart, who commanded the 79th Armoured Division, the "funnies" were modified tanks adapted from Sherman and Churchill designs specifically for D-Day. Their job was to provide armored support for the first wave of troops as they landed on the beaches. The first funnies to land were U.S.-designed duplex-drive tanks (DDs). They were launched out at sea and "swam" to the beach using a propellor and a skirt for flotation. Once on land, they operated normally. Other funnies had flails of twirling chains that were used to clear mines. Other variations included the modified Churchill AVRE, or Armoured Vehicle, which could be fitted with a bunker-busting mortar, a bulldozer, a metal carpet layer, a folding bridge, a ditch-filler, or a flame-thrower.

Mortar – a large gun that fires shells in a high arc.

07:25 hours

Guided into position by the midget submarine X-23, the first assault waves are closing in on the beach by 06:30 hours. LCTs (Landing Craft, Tank) carrying the DD tanks are in the lead.

07:25 hours

The tanks have to be launched 5,000 yards (4,575 m) from the beach because of rough seas. The LCTs soon catch up and pass the tanks. At least one tank is hit and sinks.

07:45 hours

Despite the rough seas, 28 out of 40 tanks make it safely onto the beach and go straight into action. By now, all the German positions have been silenced by assault units from the East Yorks and South Lancs regiments.

EYEWITNESS: William Lloyd, private, East Yorkshire Regiment

"Bullets just came at you like raindrops. You could hear them whistling and passing you and hitting the ground near you but you just kept going on. It was a gradual sloping beach, hadn't much to give us any cover. A few sand dunes and things like that but apart from that we hadn't much cover at all."

08:30 hours

A second wave of assault units begin to land. By mid-morning, the South Lancs have secured Hermanville, while the East Yorks have made it to the southern outskirts of Ouistreham. Back on the beach, three brigades are trying to land and move inland over one surfaced road to the assembly areas at Hermanville. The result is heavy congestion and a three-hour delay. Further east, the advance also stalls around Colleville. South of the village, the Suffolks come up against the HQ of the 736th Infantry Regiment. The strongpoint is manned by 300 men, and takes until 20:00 hours to clear.

Allied troops take cover from German snipers and machine guns.

13:30 hours

British commandos under Lord Lovat seize Hermanville.

16:00 hours

Tanks of the 27th Armored Brigade have made it through the Hermanville traffic jams.

Midget submarine – a small submersible with a crew of one or two.

Their arrival is none too soon: the 21st Panzer Division launches the only German armored counterattack of D-Day.

19:00 hours

Panzers are in Lion-sur-Mer and for two hours the Allied invasion force is split in two. However, the German forces cannot exploit the position.

21:00 hours

Hundreds of Allied gliders are seen overhead. Colonel Rauch, the Panzer battle group commander, assumes their goal is Caen.

Defeated German prisoners are marched into Allied territory.

Knowing he has no support and facing a vast invasion fleet, Rauch decides to pull back to Bieville. The appearance of the gliders has ended the only chance the Germans will have to force the Allies back to the sea.

Additional vehicles and equipment are moved onto Sword Beach.

NIGHTFALL

Nearly 29,000 troops have landed at Sword and the D-Day objectives have been largely secured. At Caen, there has already been one German panzer attack to hold the town with more to come. Caen—a key invasion objective—is already looking like a hard nut to crack.

STRATEGY AND TACTICS: 21st Panzer Division

After serving successfully in North Africa, the 21st Panzer Division had reformed and had been sent to Normandy. On D-Day it was the only German unit in position to counterattack the Allies. But the ongoing disagreement between Rommel and von Rundstedt meant that it was based outside Caen, too far from the beaches to be able to respond immediately. Its objectives were split: to try to block the invasion on the beaches, but also to guard the routes inland. To make the best of a bad situation, the division was split up; three battalions attacked the seaborne invasion, but despite stopping the Allied progress it suffered a decisive strategic defeat. With no back-up, the 21st Panzer Division ended the day knowing the war was as good as lost.

Strategic – related to an overall campaign or war, not the immediate action.

TURNING POINTS:
The Mulberry Harbors

In great secrecy, two floating harbors were built in pieces in Great Britain, then assembled off the Normandy coast. Each dock had 6 miles (9.6 km) of flexible steel roadway floating on steel or concrete pontoons. Huge concrete blocks and sunken ships were used to make a breakwater to shelter them. They provided a vital means of bringing ashore the vast amount of men and equipment needed in the days following D-Day. Mulberry A, off Omaha Beach, was destroyed by storms on June 19. Mulberry B was moored off Arromanches at Gold Beach and proved extremely effective.

JUNE 7, D+1, English Channel

U-boats from the Biscay ports and Brittany try to break into the English Channel to attack the Western Task Force. They are stopped by patrol aircraft of the Coastal Command.

D+1, Normandy

The Allied air forces are faced with increased German air activity. German fighters make about 250 sorties over the beachheads, while there are 50 fighter-bomber attacks on the Sword area.

D+1, HMS *Faulknor*

General Bradley meets Montgomery onboard. Their meeting is dominated by what to do about the Omaha landings. The bridgehead is only 1 mile (1.6 km) deep and V Corps is still in danger of being pushed back into the sea. Collin's VII Corps at Utah is told to concentrate its efforts south toward Isigny and Carentan in order to take the pressure off Omaha. Eisenhower also meets Montgomery onboard. He is concerned that the build-up of men and equipment at the beachhead is already behind schedule. The sea is becoming rougher by the hour, meaning there is little chance of getting extra men and equipment onto the beaches.

Merchant ships are deliberately sunk to create a breakwater.

D+1, Mulberry Harbors

The first convoys of "Gooseberry" blockships arrive off Omaha Beach.

D+1, German Defenses

After having been initially taken by surprise on June 6, the German Army in France begins to organize to fight back.

D+1, Utah

VII Corps HQ assigns the task of capturing Carentan to the 101st Airborne.

D+1, Omaha

The position of Colonel Rudder's Rangers at Pointe du Hoc is perilous. Fewer than 100 men have survived and they have been pushed back

Breakwater – a barrier built to protect a coast from the force of the waves.

to a strip of cliff only 200 yards (182 m) wide. Fresh supplies of food, water and ammunition are delivered but the Rangers must hold on until the 116th can reach them.

D+1, Gold

The 50th is making good progress. By noon, two battalions of the 56th Brigade have entered Bayeux unopposed.

D+1, Juno

A reinforced panzergrenadier regiment of the 12th SS Panzer Division attacks the Canadians. They push them back 3 miles (5 km). The 12th SS Panzer Division begins to arrive in force and concentrates west of Caen. The British Second Army loses another chance to close on the town.

German prisoners are loaded onto a transport ship to sail to England.

The numbers of Ju-88s had been reduced by Allied bombing raids.

8 JUNE, D+2, English Channel

German air raids on the invasion fleet continue.

D+2, Mulberry Harbors

The last "Gooseberry" blockships are sunk in position to form the fixed breakwaters of the two floating harbors: Mulberry A off Ste Laurent on Omaha Beach and Mulberry B off Arromanches on Gold Beach.

D+2, Great Britain

In London, General Eisenhower holds his first press conference since June 6.

EYEWITNESS: Claude J. Mercer, U.S. 29th Field Artillery Battalion

"Went into Ste-Mere-Eglise. Tank battle going on. Flame throwers. Saw a German soldier, a 'human torch,' crawl to the center of the street when a Panzer rolled right over him, squashing him flat and extinguishing the flames at the same time. American tanks destroyed most of the German tanks, for the loss of three of their own. Saw a sunken road north of the town which the German tanks had used and also crushed some of their own dead."

Blockship – a ship that is deliberately sunk to create an obstacle.

A U.S. patrol moves cautiously past the churchyard in St Marcouf.

EYEWITNESS: H.S. Gillies, colonel, King's Own Scottish Borderers

"We had barely crossed the start-line when the enemy reacted fiercely, with well-sited machine-guns and intense mortar fire which enfiladed (fired sideways along) the companies as they moved forward. It was almost reminiscent of some First World War battlefield. We could see the tracer bullets flicking off the corn."

D+2, Utah
Regiments of the 90th Division come ashore to join the lead elements that have been coming ashore since D+1.

D+2, Omaha
The U.S. 2nd Infantry Division comes ashore. Its lead regiments, the 9th and 38th Infantry, are immediately rushed forward into the center of V Corps' lines.

D+2, Gold
The British 56th Brigade consolidates its position in Bayeux, pushing southwest to block any German advance from St Lô.

D+2, Juno
The Canadian advance south of the Caen–Bayeux rail line is stopped by a counterattack by elements of the 12th SS Panzer Division moving west.

JUNE 9, D+3, Omaha
General Omar Bradley comes ashore to join the HQ of the U.S. First Army, which has been established a couple of miles inland from the former Ranger positions on the Pointe du Hoc. Off Omaha, landing ships arrive carrying the bulk of the U.S. 2nd Armored Division, which has been at sea since June 7.

Part of a prefabricated Mulberry harbor is towed across the Channel.

Prefabricated – describes something that is built before being put into position.

Young German soldiers man their PAK 40 anti-tank gun.

JUNE 9, D+3, Juno and Sword

There are now believed to be three panzer divisions north of Caen—the 12th SS, Panzer Lehr and 21st Panzer—blocking a direct advance to the town.

JUNE 10, D+4, Utah

On the right flank of the bridgehead the advance north has stalled after the capture of Azeville the day before. The 22nd Infantry is meant to attack Quinéville but it is still being held by German positions at Crisbecq. Meanwhile, in the attack on Carentan, a causeway crossing is also proving an obstacle to the 101st Airborne paratroopers.

D+4, Omaha

In the center of the V Corps bridgehead, the 2nd Division succeeds in taking Trevieres in the early morning. The remains of the German 352nd Division is withdrawn to a new defensive line northwest of St Lô, allowing the 2nd Division to make an advance of over 5 miles (8 km). V Corps' beachhead is now 7 miles (11 km) wide at its deepest, a vast improvement on the situation on D+1.

D+4, Sword

East of the Orne, the Germans are keeping up the pressure on the 6th Airborne Division. At 09:00 hours German infantry begin to advance on Ranville, but they have no support and are driven off.

D+4, Beachheads

The U.S. 9th Infantry Division begins to land at Utah, while units of the U.S. 30th Infantry Division begin to land at Omaha. There are now 10 U.S. Army divisions in Normandy. In the British sector at St Croix-sur-Mer, the RAF opens its first airfield in France.

STRATEGY AND TACTICS: "Bocage" fighting

As the Allies pushed inland, efforts to break out of the peninsula were frustrated by fierce German resistance, particularly around Caen in the British-Canadian sector and St Lô in the American sector. Allied armor was held back in the bocage, the local term for a landscape of high, thick hedgerows and deep, narrow lanes, many of which had been flooded. This difficult terrain favored the German defenders, who hid behind the high hedges in their tanks. A British armored thrust at Villers-Bocage was defeated on June 13. Operation Epsom, a large-scale infantry offensive west of Caen was also defeated on June 25–29. It took several weeks of hard fighting before the Allies managed to fight their way out of the bocage and head southeast.

Tracer – ammunition coated with chemicals to make its flight visible.

Commandos set out to capture a German gun position.

D+4, Air Campaign

Ultra intelligence locates the Panzer Group West's mobile HQ 12 miles (19 km) south of Caen. Four squadrons of Typhoons attack the HQ, destroying it.

JUNE 11, D+5, Omaha

Regiments of the 2nd and 1st Divisions are regrouping south and west of the Cerisy Forest after making rapid gains. But their lack of progress today is a mistake. If they had advanced they would have moved into a 10-mile (16-km) gap north of Caumont, between the Panzer Lehr Division attacking the British south of Bayeux and the remnants of the 352nd Division northeast of St Lô.

D+5, Gold

The 7th Armored Division continues to advance slowly. The British are entering the Bocage country, where sunken lanes and thick hedgerows are proving difficult obstacles for tanks.

D+5, Juno

After the action around Le Mesnil, this part of the front stabilizes over the next two weeks.

D+5, Sword

After yesterday's heavy counterattack on the 3rd Parachute Brigade at Breville, the 5th Black Watch of the 51st Division's 153rd Brigade reinforce the frontline here.

EYEWITNESS: Sergeant Morawetz, 12th SS Panzer Division, Bretteville

"After a muffled bang and a swaying, as if a track had been ripped off, the vehicle came to a stop. At the same moment, after another explosion, it began to burn. I jumped out, then I saw flames coming out of the open hatch as if from a blow torch. To my left, other burning panzers."

A British Sherman tank crew takes a break after fighting at Benouville.

Blow torch – a device that uses gas to burn an intense flame.

TURNING POINTS: The fall of Caen

Caen controlled the Allied exit from Normandy. Hitler had ordered it to be held at all costs. Having failed to capture the city on a number of occasions since D-Day, General Montgomery was determined to succeed. On July 7, he ordered nearly 470 heavy Allied bombers to attack the northern part of the city to destroy the German defenses before a land assault on July 9. Many French civilians were killed in the bombing and much of the city was destroyed, but as the British and Canadians moved into the ruined city, the Germans started to pull out. After two days of fighting, Caen finally fell to the Allies on July 20, 1944, a month later than the invasion planners had hoped.

D+5, Paris

Von Rundstedt and Rommel meet to discuss the situation facing Seventh Army. Their conclusions are sent separately to Hitler.

JUNE 12, D+6, Beachheads

The battle has become one of logistics. A race is on to land troops and equipment faster than the Germans can bring in reinforcements.

D+6, Utah

The German defense line between Montebourg to Quinéville is cracking. In Carentan, the German garrison receives supplies, but they are too late. Surrounded on three sides by U.S. troops, the commander has already ordered his men to withdraw south. During the night, there is news of a German counterattack. Bradley orders V Corps to have tanks and armored infantry ready to stop it.

D+6, Omaha

The 2nd and 1st Divisions renew their attacks to the south and west of the Cérisy Forest and advance into the Caumont Gap.

U.S. troops clear a truck route through the ruins of a French town.

D+6, Carentan

The capture of Carentan links all the invasion beachheads for the first time.

D+7, Normandy

The Allied focus switches to breaking out of Normandy. Cherbourg falls on June 27, and St Lô and Caen on July 18. On August 1 the U.S. Third Army is activated under General Patton. Within a week it has struck west into Brittany, east to Le Mans, and south to the Loire River. The breakout has been achieved.

Logistics – support services, such as supply and transportation.

Glossary

amphibious Working on water and on land.

blitz A sustained bombing campaign against a target.

blockship A ship that is deliberately sunk to create an obstacle.

breakwater A barrier built to protect a coast from the force of the waves.

bridgehead A small foothold of land occupied in enemy territory.

bunker A buried, heavily reinforced defensive position.

causeway A raised embankment carrying a road.

congestion Blockages that cause delay.

counterattack An attack launched in response to an enemy attack.

DD tanks Duplex drive tanks, adapted to "swim" in water.

diplomacy The conduct of relations between governments.

embarkation Loading personnel and equipment onto boats.

flank The exposed side of a military formation.

French Resistance A secret organization fighting against German occupation of France.

frogman A combat swimmer with a wetsuit and breathing apparatus.

garrison A military unit defending a town or strongpoint.

glider An aircraft with no engine that travels on air currents.

landing craft Flat-bottomed boats for landing troops and supplies on beaches.

meteorologist A scientist who studies and predicts weather patterns.

midget submarine A small submersible with a crew of one or two.

mines Floating bombs that detonate when they are struck by a ship.

minesweepers Small warships whose job is to locate and destroy mines.

mortar A large gun that fires shells in a high arc.

NCO (non-commissioned officer); a junior officer promoted from the ranks.

OB West (Oberbefehlshaber West); the command of all German forces in western Europe.

paratrooper A soldier who parachutes into battle.

pathfinder A soldier who marks a landing zone or a route.

perimeter A barrier around the outside of an area of land.

radar A system for locating objects by bouncing radio waves off them.

relieve To come to the aid of a unit that is under attack.

sabotage Acts of damage that harm an enemy's war effort.

saturation bombing Heavily bombing an area, rather than a specific target.

shingle A beach made up of gravel and small pebbles.

strategic Related to an overall campaign or war, not the immediate action.

surveillance Monitoring enemy movement and communications.

tracer Ammunition that is coated in chemicals that make its flight visible.

Further resources

Books

Bliven, Bruce Jnr. *Invasion! The Story of D-Day*. Sterling Point, 2008.

Connolly, Sean. *The D-Day Landings* (Witness to History). Heinemann-Raintree, 2008.

Davenport, John C. *D-Day and the Liberation of France* (Milestones in Modern World History. Chelsea House Publications, 2010.

Drez, Ronald J. *Remember D-Day: The Plan, the Invasion, Survivor Stories*. National Geographic Children's Books, 2004.

McGowen, Tom. *D-Day: Cornerstones of Freedom*. Children's Press, 2004.

Martin, Martha. *D-Day* (Crabtree Chrome). Crabtree Publishing Company, 2012.

Miller, Terry. *D-Day: The Allies Strike Back During World War II* (24/7 Goes to War: On the Battlefield). Scholastic Library Publishing, 2009.

Murray, Doug. *D-Day: The Liberation of Europe Begins*. Rosen Publishing Group, 2008.

Platt, Richard. *D-Day Landings: The Story of the Allied Invasion* (DK Readers). DK Children, 2004.

Stein, R. Conrad. *The World War II D-Day Invasion in American History*. Enslow Publishers, 2004.

Vansant, Wayne. *Normandy: A Graphic History of D-Day, The Allied Invasion of Hitler's Fortress Europe*. Zenith Press, 2012.

Zaloga, Steven J. *The Most Daring Raid of World War II: D-Day—Pointe du Hoc* (The Most Daring Raids in History). Rosen Publishing Group, 2011.

Websites

http://www.dday.co.uk/
Tour of the Normandy Beaches as they are today.

http://www.dday.org/
National D-Day Memorial site, with a full account of U.S. participation in the landings.

http://www.army.mil/d-day/
U.S. Army site dedicated to D-Day, with photographs, maps, and accounts.

http://www.pbs.org/wgbh/amex/dday/
Site to accompany the PBS series American Experience.

http://www.history.com/topics/d-day
History.com D-Day page, with videos, articles, and photographs.

Index